Maximize Your Business ROI Scientifically

Hardcore Secrets Revealed

By

Author Name

FARID PREMANI

For suggestions, contact & consulting work contact

Email: farid@aleedex.com

www.aleedex.com

ISBN-13:978-1514178966
ISBN-10:1514178966

DEDICATION & ACKNOWLEDGEMENT

I am dedicating this book to Divine guidance who helped me achieve different missions in life whether done for profit or socially driven objectives. My family and specially my community where I got blessed with guidance from our spiritual leader His Highness Prince Karim Aga Khan following whose footsteps we got into vision for poverty alleviation and helping improvise Quality of Life of others.

In this book we have tried to empower people who want to take control over their lives and grow rich starting small reaping idea to success either starting their digital business, services or growing their small business through simple steps generating online leads.

Trust God – Take the Charge While
Rest is Simple!

TABLE OF CONTENT

ABOUT THE AUTHOR

FARID PREMANI IS A DIGITAL CONSULTANT HAVING HIS OWN HIGH GROWTH BRANDS AND SOCIAL PHILANTRHOPIST WORKING ON AREAS OF POVERTY ALLEIVATION THROUGH POWER OF TECHNOLOGY.
HE HAS BEEN TEDX SUGARLAND SPEAKER, DIGITAL AWARD WINNER IN 2015 SUMMIT AND HAVE SERVED MORE THAN 120+ CLIENTS FROM ALL DIVERSE CRITERIAS GROWING THEM FROM GARAGE TO DECENT 272% AVERAGE ROI SALES.

HE IS AUTHOR OF FOUR BOOKS, DOES DIGITAL COACHING AND

HAVE RECENTLY STARTED 501C(3) NOT FOR PROFIT NAMELY
IGNITETHESPARK.ORG – A SOCIAL NETWORK CONNECTING
ENTREPRENEURS

EMAIL HIM FOR INTEREST OR CONSULTATION AT
FARID@ALEEDEX.COM

CHAPTER 1

HOW TO BRAIN STORM IDEA AND FULLY TEST IT FOR ROLL OUT

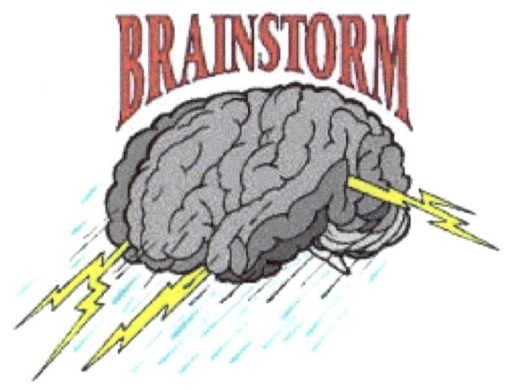

Some would-be entrepreneurs shell out ages hoping to think about "the massive idea". My very own experience suggests that massive quantities of time could be consumed looking for and debating "the significant idea" - it likely not the handiest basis stone for the excellent new company. Do not get me wrong, lots of thinking and refining time is absolutely crucial to make sure that the company strategy is as good when you could get it prior to launch. But if you might be agonizing to establish something on which to build your online business then you definitely may very well be barking up the wrong tree.

My philosophy is that any feasible organization commences by using a pain...a suffering that is afflicting your prospective purchasers. But regrettably too many bright new start-ups are based mostly upon a solution...an answer to some suffering that both does not exist, or isn't really agonizing adequate that ample individuals are heading to pay their good money to deal with it with the new remedy.

Try to steer clear of forcing yourself to come back up with "the huge idea" - you happen to be not often at your most inventive when forcing on your own to return up with "two new concepts right before bedtime" and carry up this exercise for at least 10 days with gaps and mood swings. Yes, most important write it down somewhere.

Do you know the "pains" that you simply expertise as part of your everyday life for a purchaser or with your customers? Are they adequately accepting that many others would pay really hard attained income for the solution...your answer? Talk to your pals and colleagues what are the irritations they face - in the event you do this then you have by now done your first mini bit of current market testing, congratulations!

No matter whether it's pinpointing a "pain" or creating "solutions" to that ache - except you would like to deliver the service or product in exactly the exact same way as some others are currently undertaking, then you certainly will need to complete some imagining and concepts era. Listed here can be a number of ways in which you may uncover valuable:

Here's a brainstorming approach.

• Write down your difficulty or challenge
• Open a note book wholly at random and generate down the 1st list
• Then make it possible for your mind to wander freely and publish down the main 10 words that occur to intellect by association while using the noun
• Now glimpse at your problem all over again and for every within your 10 words and phrases permit that phrase immediate your contemplating in direction of an plan to resolve the challenge and generate it down

For those who such as this tactic and want to enlist the assistance of many hundreds of barnstormers throughout the entire world then Yvonne Adele has constructed a company based in Australia named Ideasculture.com. To get a smallish fee she will place your concern out to her network and have the effects again to you personally within a day.

Springwise.com is a fantastic website which announces and provides history on new companies with new strategies. If it is on springwise.com then anyone someplace is already doing it - but perhaps there is space during the market for you too?

Halfbakery.com is really a pretty light-hearted database of primary, fictitious tips and inventions normally the end result of irritations that contributors spot inside their day-to-day life. You might attain inspiration from your absurd or you might just have a very snicker, which can in all probability help your creative imagination.

Good luck just be wise to see and create a thin line. That you research up for idea but still protect it from being stolen. Good luck!

CHAPTER 2

MIND MAPPING YOUR IDEA - CALL THINK TANK INN – BE A PRO ONE DAY ONE

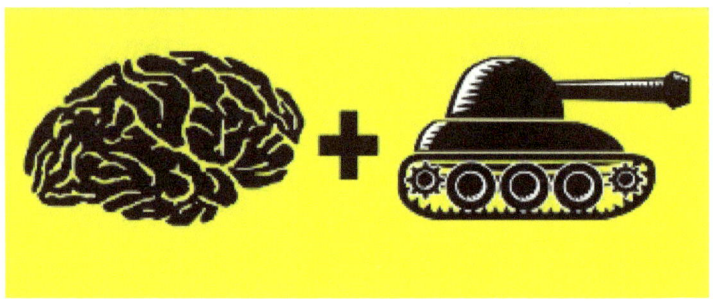

Masterminds and Imagine Tanks are sweeping the country, and many small business people need to access them as a result of their promising effects for members who choose them significantly.

For all those who require a heads up, a consider tank or mastermind is often a team of people that fulfill on a regular basis which has a dedication to thrive and access precise plans. Each member in the group works in direction of their own personal expansion and advancement when also doing work for your advancement and success of the other team members. You will find a lot additional to it than that, but this post isn't about defining what a consider tank or mastermind is. Relatively, this post is meant to aid you get ready your contemplating and state of mind for the believe tank or mastermind group, so that's what we'll have a look at below here!

Refer one of the best websites which I used to start with meetup.com try to join as many likeminded groups as possible, do attend 3 meetings a week. Set a target and network!
Eventually your mission and vision will derive you to attract likeminded people which may become your mentors, partners,

investors or someone to learn from and move on creating the master plan!

Hope you obtain quite tips from these ten suggestions!

1. Intentions

Setting correct intentions (toward self and others) with empowering and straightforward motives will help you flourish when you relate to others and when you do the operate and functions you established out to do.

2. Objectives

You must use a clear and certain purpose or simply a definite want of anything you ought to obtain. For each conference you should keep this intention in your mind, or if your aim is attained, use a new target to concentrate on.

3. Movement

In a very Consider Tank or Mastermind, it's important to arrive able to do the job and prepared to move Ahead. Forward movement may be the entire position!

4. Soreness

You have to be prepared to be at ease while becoming unpleasant. It is only once when we are challenged that we mature. In the course of your occasions, you may often experience stretched and challenged times. That is a terrific element to learn how to eat the frog and move on with life.

5. Win- Win Attitude

Once you sit within the mastermind desk yourself, come willing to be served. Your meetings need to in no way an afterthought.

6. Empowerment

Create a structure that will help you deal with emotional concerns, earlier hurts, or emotional scars. It isn't therapy. It can be additional about identifying your personal empowerment and performing from it, relocating you to definitely new levels of everyday living enrichment and achievement. Assume them before and prepare in advance!

7. Accountability

Only after we are accountable for our intentions and actions can we achieve to bigger heights. Our time and source financial investment in these a group is frequently substantial, and so very little lower than complete throttle responsibility and accountability is going to be suitable for your standard of progress and accomplishment to every member' expectations.

8. Muck

It is completely natural for any little muck and mire to come back up in your case within a Feel Tank or Mastermind, and occasionally you may even get emotional or shed tears. It is all portion with the amazing development approach. Precisely what is NOT a part of expansion is for you personally. The goal of a Consider Tank or Mastermind would be to move away from the muck and into the space of your brilliance and empowerment. You'll be able to only try this having a mentality to continually move forward. The muck is there to teach you a lesson which you take with you. The muck is not really there for wallowing!

9. Integrity

Just about every member have to issue enormously to all other associates. When it is your flip, you're going to get complete consideration and you will get pleasure from getting that person to breakthrough. If this can be your perspective and intention, you may acquire Enormously from the team if you are the main focus (and in many cases while you are not).

10. Dedication

Be on time for conferences, and do anything you may to maintain your conference dates.

CHAPTER 3

CONSULTATION WINS - JUST BEWARE WHO YOU ARE DISCUSSING YOUR IDEA WITH!

Do you sense like your lifetime must have far more that means? Does you visit a job working day soon after working day but sense like a thing is missing? Or are you outside of function and seeking to determine out how to proceed future? You were being put in this place on this planet for your explanation. Now at this moment that motive might not be apparent to you. But ideally with the end of the report you are going to have crystal clear clarity relating to your reason.

A lot of people are aware that they have got intent however they usually are not absolutely sure what their reason is, or how to bring their intent into their existence. And regrettably a lot of people never even come to feel like they've got reason. But even when your goal is hidden it can be however there. We are all born with objectives. **But you really have to unleash it.**

One of the methods you may unleash your intent is by turning out making a list and trying different things learning to see where you mind and heart follows you.

In the event you have the passion to produce a distinction within the lives of others, the center to inspire many others to triumph, along with a present of encouragement, then becoming a everyday living coach may be your upcoming purposeful stage. Becoming a life mentor can assist you to improve your daily life as well as the lives of other people.

There is absolutely no want for just about any of us to maintain our purposeful gifts hidden. Our presents had been meant to shine within the life of others. Lots of instances we don't give ourselves plenty of credit rating. We don't notice how significant our objective will be to lives for others. And we don't comprehend that we now have been blessed to create it by what some other person goes by. Just your lifetime tale on your own might help other folks inside a strong and purposeful way.

There is certainly an incredible chance that you simply already have what it will take to be a **wonderful professional or entrepreneur that World will know you for!** however , you just really don't know the way to deliver all of it together. As well as if that would seem difficult now, it seriously can be carried out effortlessly. After you are moving in alignment together with your goal factors move in a natural way and are fun and thrilling.

One your own search is completed trying different options available and you are determined then get on your way to find a coach, a mentor, someone who you feel you can consult with. But remember the best consultant is your own mind, heart and soul. So sit with your self-allowing room to settle and put your problems in empty space as to let Divine work for you.

To conclude rules for consultation are only 2:

1. Consult your field expert, who you feel can help you. You need to put some time out finding people, try linkedin.com you never know there are senior good people available to give some time out as advice mentoring you, or try websites like micromentor.com
2. Consult with yourself.

Move on…………

CHAPTER 4
FEASIBILITY AND RATE OF RETURN'S GAME!

Thousands of men and women aspiration of getting their own personal enterprise and also far more so become a productive entrepreneur. But what does it choose to realize success within the small business industry?

Among one of the most profitable business owners featured with the Forbes internet site, Wendy Lipton - Dibner explained that "The results of one's small business would entirely count on you. The only thing you could count on is your electrical power to accomplish your goal".

She shared her achievement tale in the Forbes web site and claimed that when she was young she realized an incredibly critical organization goal from her high school exercise which is always to head out, discover, arrive back and clarify how money is made in small business. This really is an aim she never forgot until eventually she manufactured hundreds of thousands for herself.

When she was already really effective, she hardly ever stopped knowing business and how it seriously functions. Gain would be the number one target in business enterprise and how you make it is an organic talent. Of course, there might be loads of suggestions presented and showed on TV and the world-wide-web but only you know the way you are going to make your income towards the major.

Try to ponder on these notes when pondering of a company:

1.) Passion. Organization might be set on profit even so the main of one's company ought to be anything you love. Enthusiasm counts quite a bit in firms for the reason that furthermore, it builds your determination in achieving your purpose.

2.) Effects. Business enterprise is really a major and aggressive globe, what will matter is the way you produce a difference towards your industry. How your organization will affect your industry. The financial gain within your business enterprise will rely over the influence within your enterprise. The mark it can depart on your buyers could make it increase.

3.) Profit

The last and third guideline is the bread and butter of one's enterprise. When income is not accomplished, organization will die its organic death. Do not forget that profit is your number one target. Exactly what is small business without revenue? Income will make your business stay and survive. The absence of profit implies the death of any company pursuit.

The target in company should be to earn a living. Although the achievements of your respective enterprise will rely upon the impact it's going to give towards your consumers and also to the whole world. You could be earning, your organization could have revenue but if it isn't going to undertaking influence then you certainly are only yet another ordinary entrepreneur.

Normal business people make money although successful business owners go away affect and touch life.

Feasibility of your Business enterprise Thought

Is your business strategy a superb one particular?
Analyze the organization thought
Sector examination
Aggressive benefit evaluation
Financial feasibility evaluation
Is your business notion a superb just one?

There is no magic reply to this concern. Experience has shown that a lot of the most bizarre concepts ,including the thought of the own computer have was prosperous businesses, although some have not.

It's crucial that you look critically and impartially at your company thought when figuring out whether it truly is truly worth investing your time and cash. It might be difficult to continue to be neutral about an strategy you are captivated with, so discuss to some enterprise advisor to secure a capable and aim standpoint.

When you can find no guarantees that your business will realize success, a feasibility research will assist you to determine irrespective of whether your strategy is likely to make a income ahead of you make a financial dedication.

It really is essential to do not forget that exactly what is viewed as feasible might differ drastically from person to man or woman based on the return on financial investment they want plus the danger they're prepared to acquire on.

Within your feasibility study it is best to analyses your online business strategy, industry and aggressive edge together with the economic feasibility with the business.

Analyze the company concept

During this very first stage of the feasibility analyze you would like to appear objectively within the concept and decide its profitability. This goal examination would include:

assessing the marketplace size;
assessing the competitive benefit of your thought;
acquiring independent endorsement on the concept;
evaluating funds prerequisites;
thinking of your management skill; and
checking out if anyone else has attempted your organization strategy, and when they unsuccessful - why?
Current market investigation

The moment you've got decided you will find there's market for the product or service you might be intending to offer, you need to perform some more exploration which should involve the next:

Desire investigation: In this article you determine the type of demand from customers that exists on your service or product (e.g.: client, distributor), and create the dimensions of the industry and its development ability.

Provide examination: Search at the everyday living cycle of the business. Could it be the ideal time for you to be coming into it? Also study the best way the marketplace is structured and consider about how that should influence your enterprise.

Partnership evaluation: How can the different groups throughout the field interact? What is the bargaining energy of customers and suppliers? Is there a menace of substitute goods or new entrants? Aggressive edge examination

Now that you have set up that the strategy is actually an excellent a single which you will find there's marketplace for anything you are offering, you would like to determine what helps make your service or product specific. Talk to you these queries:

How is my service or product distinctive to those provided by my competitors?

Why will customers purchase the products or services from me instead of my competition?
Are there any barriers to me coming into the market?

What helps make my competition thriving?
Economic feasibility investigation

The ultimate section within your analyze really should tackle the economic feasibility with the company concept which entails the following:

Planning an income forecast;
Estimating start-up and dealing capital necessities;
Estimating profitability; and
Examining financial viability.

And finally make it ready to pitch your investor, your friends, or family members. Remember the giant company as of today Alibaba was also started with pool of funds obtained from friends and family. So don't be shy to put your savings on side and ask for help.

Be scientific with people and there are always loads of cash available on face or sideways. Once again Trust yourself Trust your God!

CHAPTER 5
MAKE YOUR MASTER PLAN

Step #1: Identify Critical Success Factors

Critical success factors (CSFs) are a set of concise statements, usually bullet points, that represent what the organization must accomplish in order to achieve its mission. The list should include no more than 8 items, each expressing a single theme. CSFs cannot be thought of as actions, "how-tos", nor as directly manageable. Together, they represent the conditions, which if achieved, will guarantee that the organization will accomplish its mission and achieve maximum success.

Step #2: Identify Major Action-Initiatives
The action-initiatives are the specific tasks that must be carried out in order to achieve the critical success factors. They are actions that define the "how to" of achieving the organization's mission and are directly manageable and measurable. Each action-initiative must have a significant and direct impact upon at least one of the critical success factors. They are the means by which the organization can achieve the critical success factors.

Step #3: Sequence the Action-Initiatives

It is not possible to implement all initiatives at the same time. A common management error is trying to do everything at once and, consequently, not doing anything well. It is necessary to achieve excellence and closure on fewer projects rather than attempting to do everything at once. Finding that balance in a competitive and demanding environment is not easy.

Step #4: Complete an Simple Action Matrix

Across the top are critical success factors and down the left side are the action-initiatives. The action-initiatives should be entered on the chart in the order in which each will be initiated.

Step #5: Establish Accountability

Once the priority and sequencing of initiatives has been determined, it is necessary to establish accountability by assigning a "champion" to each. The champion is a member of the management team who assumes primary responsibility for the accomplishment of that particular initiative.

Step #6: Clarify Project Parameters

Although primary accountability for each action initiative resides with one member of the leadership team, all team members continue to share responsibility for its success.

Step #7: Commissioning Project Teams

The champion and perhaps a few other members of the leadership team meet with the individuals participating on the project team to orient them to the purpose, parameters and scope of the initiative. They review with them the purpose, desired outcomes, resources, constraints, etc. of the project and how this project fits with the overall strategy and direction of the business as a whole. The project team, working within the parameters established by the senior leadership team, is responsible for further planning and implementation of the project.

CHAPTER 6
YOUR MOTIVATION BOMB

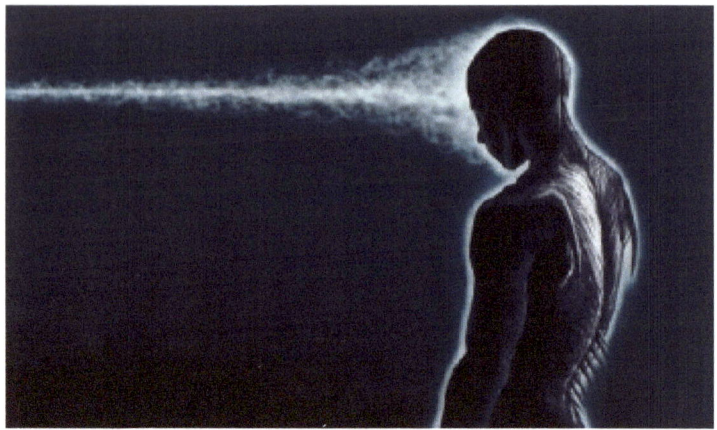

All of us know another person that has talked about pursuing his or her aspiration "one day"... could that someone be you?

What stops us from pursuing our goals? What retains us procrastinating?

1) Not Ample Funds

The number 1 cause we don't go after our desires. We need money to dwell day-to-day, plus the price of living for most "developed" nations is considerable. We are taught that cash + belongings = good results. We have been encouraged to go into debt to get the factors we would like. We use credit rating to purchase cars and trucks, households, household furniture, education and learning, and vacations. It is the typical tactic within our modern society. After we ponder pursuing our desires, we marvel how can we afford to pay for it? Starting off a little something new, similar to a organization, heading back again to high school, will require funds to create and improve, we are going to probably end making the cash we're used to, and it'll take a while to recoup the money used to make the alter. As being a result, our personal debt may perhaps maximize, although we however have our current debt load and our day-to-day living charges (and maybe supporting family members users).

2) Getting the easy Way

It is easy to try and do what every person else does. We don't have to figure out everything new. We head over to faculty, have got a vocation, receive a home, possess a household, and program for retirement. Daily life can be tough or monotonous from time to time, but it truly is predictable and comprehended. You will find a lot to get stated for adhering to the group this means you really don't stand out, and so it does not truly feel like you are swimming upstream. This route is nicely worn and straightforward to adhere to.

3) We are Afraid of Becoming Different

YOU KNOW YOUR BUSINESS
IS IN TROUBLE WHEN...

Judgment is often a major component of our lives. It starts off early. As a baby we have been in comparison to other people. There exists competitiveness in school, sporting activities, hobbies, work, and comparisons together with the car or truck we push or what neighborhood we reside in. So we conform. We do our greatest to slot in. We do not desire to truly feel unique. We wish to truly feel similar to a element of the neighborhood. So we chat about typical societal subjects: the weather, our subsequent holiday, how the kids are, the task, sports, TV shows or flicks. Fit in, and do not converse about or do everything that could "rock the boat". Pursuing our aspiration would make us sense distinct compared to the norm.

So what is it possible to do to solve this dilemma?

1) **Build the money You need**

Start out by simplifying your daily life; purchase a lot less things, decrease your expenditures, cook dinner in your house, ditch the TV, obtain a scaled-down home, get rid of your vehicle, or get an more mature auto or be part of a vehicle share, experience a bike or take the bus. Reduce or do away with your debt. Make a 6-month and 1-year prepare to avoid wasting the money you would like, and stick to your strategy.

2) **Just take Tiny Steps over the Path Much less Trodden**

By having tiny, workable measures in the direction of your targets, you might improve your confidence and build your inspiration. So go through some textbooks, get courses, or make a journey to your area in which your aspiration is now alive (consider work/volunteer holidays). If you'd like to generally be an author - get started producing, a painter - commence portray. You'll be able to get it done, however it will get time. Discovering everything new requires exercise, patience and persistence. Keep in mind studying to journey your bike, tying your shoelaces, or enjoying an instrument? It's going to take time for you to become skilled at a little something new. Be mild on by yourself.

3) **Be Diverse**

Uncover your tribe. Uncover individuals that may relate to the aspiration. Surround oneself with supporters, not detractors. Be part of local meet-up teams, Fb teams, and websites with people that have equivalent passions. Within just these teams you will discover camaraderie, encouragement, enthusiasm, and inspiration. You will share successes and problems in a safe atmosphere, a single with no judgment, which can be very important for taking favorable techniques to your dream.

The primary recommendation is usually to get started now. Halt procrastinating. There will never ever be described as a "perfect time" to start

CHAPTER 7
INSPIRING TO LEARN – IMPROVE EVERY DAY

Globalization and advancements in engineering have produced the world a far more aggressive spot. Absolutely everyone needs to keep up using the growing pace and rate in an ecosystem where transform is usually a norm. To keep up with the difficult occasions and also your peers, you have to self-understand the tactics on self-improvement to make certain that you simply stay forward on the video game. Like many people, chances are you'll have desperately required to alter your life for your greater. You could have tried out various situations and learned how challenging it was without having some guidance and path.

Self-improvement is attaining reputation at an unprecedented speed. The appearance in the world wide web suggests that people could possibly get access to numerous guidelines and concepts immediately. Most of they are accessible free of charge. Are they trusted? You will also find the standard particular progress workshops and seminars which provide a plethora of equipment to help you achieve your plans. Numerous adverts pushing the non-public development teaching programs are a draw. Though these are definitely handy, they might not be sustainable merely mainly because most individuals will not adhere to up. Without the need of the hand holding, it really is nearly unachievable to thrive.

Self enhancement can protect a wide facet of one particular particular daily life. It may possibly vary from private abilities, occupation, partnership, family members, wellness, finances, exercise, or nearly anything that may be necessary to get over the boundaries with your lifestyle.

The thought of self-improvement may differ from one particular to a different. Finally there need to be obviously described targets. These are generally the targets that a single ought to set ahead of 1 should really commence the journey of self-advancement. It should really comprise the two the short phrase aims at the same time as extended expression objectives. The linkage has to be proven.

Placing the plans it is actually under no circumstances a straightforward process. A good deal of individuals will not be confident the things they choose to boost or that they're confused with quite a few areas of self-improvement. Even though they are positive, they might not understand how to go about performing it. And triggering them to procrastinate.

A successful self-advancement journey starts with defining the plans you need to attain. Take into consideration your present-day circumstance and what you wish being more in the future. In other words, do up a roadmap of your lifetime. Understand that this roadmap is rarely mounted or long lasting. You ought to retain refining it while you go together - although not each time when one thing goes erroneous. Refocus in your new strategy and continue around the route of self-excellence to become a happier and even more fulfilled human being using a feeling of objective in life.

Ask yourself exactly what are the belongings you need to enhance to get for your vision. Produce a record and prioritize it. Make use of the Pareto Principle or maybe the 80/20 rule to rank them accordingly. Usually do not let your self be overwhelmed and frustrated by earning a lot of key modifications in the existence. This is often to permit you to definitely concentrate around the key types.

Consider your profession as an example. Just about all people expend their main waking hours on the work except you're the number of lucky kinds that do not really have to get the job done. Then work may be the significant element of the existence. Could be the present-day career driving your lifetime or even the other way spherical? Are you currently looking ahead to operate day to day or will you be just tolerating it. Does one go property daily sensation a way of accomplishment or weary and rundown?

For anyone who is sad with the position, do not allow it drag. Recognize the parts of self-advancement which you require to open up oneself to extra prospects. Triumph over the panic of failure by just taking action. Go ahead and take motion to list down the belongings you want to try and do to obtain out of this rut. You only have a single existence and why don't you enable or not it's an satisfying 1.

Concentration is without doubt one of the critical expertise which you need to have. That is about self-worth, self-assurance and self-willpower. Regardless of how frantic and exactly how lots of interruptions you have, you should not allow it divert you absent from a goals.

How committed are you presently in your ambitions? Most people think that they're committed. However they can't give a clear reply. Motivation is not just in the mind but from the coronary heart and fingers. Then to accomplish the productive consequence, then 1 should completely committed. To do that, the ideal guess is always to construct the behavior.

Inculcating the behavior for self-improvement will allow one particular to achieve the end result rapidly and properly as one particular is captivated with the journey. To put it differently, it's important to adore whatever you do should you wish to be profitable. You might be determined and may be pushed to get motion no matter what time from the day it can be. For those who desire to obtain fantastic success inside your lifetime, you must really like everything you really need to do.

By doing everything you really like, you might have the all-natural push that keeps you inspired in the journey in everyday life. Drive will probably be the key to realize good results. As a rule, you will be astonished with all your functionality and ability which you earlier believed not possible.

Are you presently ready to invest at the very least half an hour each day to master about self enhancement every single day? Continual finding out is necessary and is not always an uncomplicated course of action since it's going to take time for you personally to improve, nurture and expand. On the other hand, this can be most likely the greatest investment of one's time. Have you ever ponder simply how much have you ever spend on self-improvement? Have you ever measured the returns? The returns is usually incredible.

So, go forth and construct the muse within just you to tackle the long run complications. Use a eyesight and chart your life roadmap. An old proverb states, "Vision with no action can be a Daydream, Action without vision is often a Nightmare". Make the approach and acquire action. Keep in mind, be dedicated in reaching terrific achievements, and really like whatever you do. Continue on to boost yourself to the superior. These are definitely the inspiration which you will need within your journey to private accomplishment.

CHAPTER 8

E-WORLD TIPS TO ENTER AN ONLINE BUSINESS

Anyone, from beginner to seasoned on-line entrepreneur, can advantage from this process in mastering how to start off a business on the net.

Move one: Look for a need and fill it
Many people that are just starting out make the error of looking for a product 1st, as well as industry 2nd.

To spice up your chances of results, begin using a market place.
The trick will be to look for a group of people that are exploring for any resolution to your dilemma, but not obtaining many effects. The online market place tends to make this sort of marketplace study quick:

Pay a visit to on-line boards to view what questions persons check with and what issues they are hoping to resolve

.

Do search phrase exploration to locate search phrases that a lot of people are searching, but for which not numerous web-sites are competing.

Check out your opportunity competitors by checking out their sites and having notice of what they're executing to fill the desire. Then you definitely can use what you've got acquired and generate a product for just a marketplace that now exists--and do it much better compared to the competitors.

Step two: Generate copy that sells
There's a tested gross sales copy components that requires site visitors by means of the selling process from your instant they get there to your minute they create a purchase:

Arouse fascination by using a powerful headline.
Describe the trouble your solution solves.
Set up your trustworthiness as a solver of the problem.
Incorporate testimonies from persons who've employed your products.
Speak about the merchandise and just how it positive aspects the person.
Make an offer.
Produce a robust ensure.
Produce urgency.
Question to the sale.
All through your copy, you must aim on how your item or support is uniquely in a position address people's challenges or make their life greater. Feel similar to a purchaser and inquire "What's in it for me?"

Stage three: Style and develop your website
Once you've obtained your industry and product, and you have nailed down your offering process, now you happen to be prepared for your small-business website design. Remember to maintain it very simple. You have got less than 5 seconds to seize someone's attention--otherwise they are gone, hardly ever to get seen once more. Some important tips to have in mind:

Select one or two simple fonts on the white qualifications.

Make your navigation distinct and simple, as well as the same on each and every page.

Only use graphics, audio or video clip when they greatly enhance your concept.

Include things like an opt-in supply in order to collect e-mail addresses.

Ensure it is uncomplicated to buy--no in excess of two clicks concerning opportunity buyer and checkout.

Your site is you're on the web storefront, so enable it to be customer-friendly.

Step four: Use engines like google to drive qualified prospective buyers in your site

Pay-per-click promotion will be the best method of getting traffic to some brand-new web-site. It's two benefits over awaiting the website traffic to return to you organically. Initial, PPC advertisements display up about the lookup pages immediately, and next, PPC advertisements permit you to take a look at different keywords and phrases, too as headlines, selling prices and selling ways. Not merely would you get quick targeted visitors, but you may also use PPC advertisements to find your best, highest-converting key terms. You then can distribute the search phrases through your web site as part of your copy and code, which is able to support your rankings within the organic and natural search results.

Build an expert status for yourself
People today utilize the world-wide-web to discover data. Offer that data without cost to other web sites, and you will see much more traffic

and better online search engine rankings. The secret is to usually incorporate a link to your web site with each tidbit of data.

Give absent absolutely free, skilled content material. Produce posts, videos or some other written content that folks will find beneficial. Distribute that material by means of on the web posting directories or social networking web pages.

Consist of "send to some friend" inbound links on worthwhile articles in your web-site.

Become an active expert in market boards and social networking internet sites wherever your concentrate on market hangs out.

You are going to access new readers. But a lot better, each web site that posts your content material will connection back to yours. Search engines like yahoo like backlinks from suitable internet sites and may reward you from the rankings.

Use the electric power of e-mail marketing to show guests into consumers.

Once you develop an opt-in record, you're creating a person of the most precious property of one's web based business. Your shoppers and subscribers have specified you permission to send out them e-mail. Meaning:

You might be supplying them one thing they've asked for.
You are building life time associations with them.
The reaction is 100 percent measurable.
E-mail marketing and advertising is less costly and much more effective than print, Tv set or radio since it can be very qualified.
Any individual who visits your website and opts in towards your checklist is an extremely sizzling guide. And there's no superior software than e-mail for next up with these prospects.

Improve your revenue through back-end sales and upselling

One of your most critical net marketing and advertising tactics is usually to establish each and every customer's life time worth. At the very least 36 percent of people that have ordered from you as soon as will get from you all over again if you comply with up with them. Closing that to start with sale is definitely quite possibly the most complicated part-- not to say the most costly. So use back-end advertising and upselling to get them to purchase once again:

Present products that complement their initial obtain.
Send out electronic loyalty discount coupons they could redeem on their own upcoming check out.
Supply similar items with your "Thank You" website page right after they acquire.

Reward your customers for their loyalty and they're going to grow to be all the more loyal.

Finally take some time out to get niche sites where your customers are present, for an auto dealer it may be auto traders, car gurus, Craig list. For pet lovers it may be pet social networks, for recruiter it may be linked in and take some time out to post your products and see the response. First work with organic free versions and then try out some paid – But most important of all, don't forget to gauge your return on investment as this is the only tool which will help you learn what do you invest to get what return from which channels. And trust me your investors will love you for this. Good luck!

CHAPTER 9

HOW TO BEAT YOUR COMPETITION WITH BETTER DEALS

37 Rules to register in your mind. Short and Sweet but Refer back so you at least remember them and apply!

1. Better quality/longer-lasting

A great one to fight off the price wars, because it makes a higher price justified. Plus, your smallness means you can put in that extra bit of TLC that really makes a better-quality product shine.

2. Rarer

Sick of seeing the same mass-marketed products everywhere you go? So are we. Give the Ikea effect the cold shoulder by offering something your customers can't buy anywhere else.

3. Easier to use

Just keep it simple? If a customer can figure out how to use your super-hydro-manu-sizer-gizmo in two seconds rather than two hours, you've got the edge.

4. Safer to use

This is a particularly strong one if your customers are likely to have kids - or if they are kids. It might take a bit of user testing, and it's worth getting an accreditation, but believe us, it'll work. No one wants to end up decapitated by the less-safe tin opener on the supermarket shelves to save a few pennies.

5. More efficient

Does your product get more done than its rivals? Is it quicker? Easier to set up and dissemble? Bonanza. Speed, these days, is ever more of the essence - and it's an incredibly powerful sales tool.

6. More compact

Never underestimate effect. The maker of this mini-torch made their millions simply by shrinking the humble torch. Make it pocket-size, easier to carry and transport.

7. Waterproof

Apply some common sense here: this will obviously depend on what your product's used for.

8. More retro

Remember when that massive comeback? It played on the retro effect.

Old is the new. If your target customers are under 30, over 50, or trendy, they'll appreciate the novelty of retro.

9. More modern
Of course, that leaves the 31 - 49-year-old bracket wide open. Either them, or anyone remotely interested in technology, cutting-edge design, or the like.

10. Design that is more
beautiful/quirky/fun/edgy/stylish/simple/patterned/non-patterned/etc We'll give our backslash key a break - you get the idea. Something as seemingly superficial as appearance can dramatically alter a customer's perception of its worth.

11. More beautiful/quirky/etc packaging
Ah packaging, the marketing executive's closest ally. The power of packaging allows you to dress up any product to the price point you want.

12. Designed by someone cool or endorsed by a celebrity
Not easy to secure, but very powerful. Think celebrity perfumes - they might smell like molten plastic, but they sell like hotcakes.

13. Quieter
Applies to any product that makes noise when used, with the exception of speakers (especially subwoofers). Noise is annoying. Eradicate for customer zen - which equals repeat custom.

14. Fresher/tastier/healthier/more organic

If you sell food or drink, you can do what the supermarkets can't. You can make things on-the-spot, preservative-free, and downright delicious. Do it.

15. Greener/more ethical

Whether it's recycled, recyclable, or in some small way helps the plight of Tibetan goat farmers, it taps into the biggest consumer trend to hit the middle class since Boden.

16. Sourced in Britain/locally sourced/home-made

This holds ever-greater sway, not just because it cuts emissions, but also because people increasingly want to know where their stuff has come from.

17. Approved by a respected organization

This holds similar kudos to celebrity endorsement, albeit probably with a different crowd. Jump through the hoops of a trade or standards organization and then stick their approval seal on every bit of marketing material you've got.

18. Not tested on animals

This holds sway with plenty of non-veggies, so it's well worth shouting about.

19. More daring

Sex still sells. And as a small business, you can take far more risks than a large company confined by 50-year-old policies. Risqué appeals to a far-wider net of consumer than you might ever have imagined.

Your service!!!

20. **Better customer service**

This is such an easy one - and it's free. Smile, be polite, build relationships with your customers and respond to complaints quickly and calmly. It's that simple. But it's something big companies find impossible to do well.

21. **More favorable opening hours**

Whether you go 24/7 or just open Saturdays when your rivals are shut, making a customer's life more convenient and shaping your business around their lifestyle is guaranteed to bring them through the doors.

22. **Faster delivery**

Hire a crew of Hell's Angels if need be, because this one can make or break a buying decision for time-poor customers.

23. Offer online ordering where competitors don't

As we said, convenience is a number one priority for an ever-growing number of consumers these days. So let them buy your products while they're browsing the web at work - and get sales coming in 24/7 too.

24. Your website is more efficient/reliable/quicker/simpler

We can't say it enough: websites are key these days. Get a good one, and you look professional and encourage people to get on there all the time. Read more here on how to get it spot-on.

25. Offer freebies that competitors don't

This can be something as simple - but as utterly charming - as offering customers a cup of tea. It really does make all the difference.

26. Being country-wide or international

A broader reach will win you more customers and give you an edge over those who only deliver down the road. It takes a lot of organization and careful management, but can work wonders.

27. The gender or age of employees. Should be right for the audience. Study them and their needs.

28. Employees' expertise

The best salespeople are those who know their subject matter inside-out. As a small business, you can nail this one, because you're most likely to employ people with a good dose of passion for what you're doing. Use it: train staff to know your product and be happy to explain it in-depth and make recommendations. Think of the service you get in independent wine shop for inspiration.

29. **Employees wear uniform**

A small thing, but a powerful one. It makes your business look more professional and trustworthy, which can go a very long way.

Your business

30. **No frills deals**

Some people like it straight-up. Take a leaf out of Ryanair's book, or just strip down your premises and packaging to their bare minimum to appeal to time-poor, fuss-free individuals.

31. **Loads of frills deals**

Of course, for every minimalist there is a, um, maximize. Chuck in lots of complimentary bits and bobs, pamper your customers, and make packaging nice and froufrou.

32. Wider range of products

Variety is the spice of life - but that doesn't mean your shelves need to rival Tesco's. Go niche, then go broad within your specialism. If you have more trowels than B&Q, the gardeners will come to you.

33. Better payment options

This is a difficult one if you're an early-stage business because cash flow is so key to your survival, but if you're longer-established and have enough in the bank to allow a 100-day payment period, you have a big edge over more stringent companies.

34. Better located

That can mean nearer public transport, or with parking facilities, right through to having a beautiful view. Or simply being the first of your kind in an area. Location, location, location applies just as much to commercial premises as private property.

35. More pleasant premises

Whether you go for a super-sweet old-fashioned tea-shop vibe, a vibrant wall mural, or ultra-chic interior design, surroundings market the experience. Make your premises memorable and beautiful, and customers will want to come back.

36. Having an outdoors

Sell food and drink? Have a garden or a pavement? Great - you've just doubled your covers for every single month of summer. And winter too, if you get a gas heater and a couple of pretty lamps.

37.   Being charitable

Put in an hour or two a week at your local old people's home, donate 5% of your profits to charity, sponsor the local kids' football team - anything along these lines, modestly publicized, will win customers' hearts.

CHAPTER 10
CONSISTENCY IS THE KING

"Take reliable motion every single working day or possibly a calendar year from now... component of your perception will likely have died." -

Regularity.

Dictionary.com describes regularity as "steadfast adherence towards the identical principles, training course, variety." that sounds great and all, but how can that utilize in true everyday living? Probably you've wondered what that means for your personal existence also. Regularity is a thing which I accustomed to believe that I struggled with... the truth was which I was just in keeping with the incorrect issue.

Increasing up with CF, consistency was something that came easy. Daily sure points needed to take place - do breathing treatments, acquire pills, do everything doable not to get sick. Accomplishing most of these tasks within the similar time every day made it a lot much easier to live a standard lifestyle. But then... the adult many years arrived, and with them arrived the brand new challenge of juggling the consistency of caring for my wellbeing with going immediately after my dreams in the very same time. This is where the ball acquired dropped.

As an alternative to discovering to get consistent while in the new region of heading immediately after my destiny, I created the selection to surrender on my dreams and give in into the regularity of lifetime - no matter what our circumstances are, we were not built to give up and provides in to illness, credit card debt, poor relationships, or whatever messes manage to abide by us all over. Simply because our overall health calls for somewhat little bit far more treatment than the typical "normal" individual, that doesn't signify we will not constantly go after our dreams. These are there for just a explanation and no matter whether we are living in illness or in wellbeing, our desires are meant to be lived instead of just dreamed.

Properly, I had been infamous for regularly obtaining big goals after which sitting over the couch waiting for them to occur. Each working day views of what can be popped into my head and like clock do the job, they continuously obtained brushed aside by the tiny gremlins on my shoulder that screamed "you are not able to do this - you're absolutely nothing but a sick individual destined to die youthful! Halt dreaming! Quit making an attempt! Stop trying! Give in! Just hook you as much as your vest and do your respiration procedure yet again and Prevent DREAMING!"

It is really sort of funny to think how consistent I used to be with entertaining this kind of lies! The lies finally turned so unpleasant that a transform required to come about. That modify started by using a choice. When the final decision was created being per entertaining thoughts of daily life and regularly accomplishing the get the job done to get to my desires even though remaining balanced, my whole everyday living adjusted! Have you been in keeping with the wrong detail too? For those who have, it is alright - once in a while we all get astray. Here is my obstacle for you at this time:

Choose out a pen and paper. Jot down everything you would love to have happen inside the upcoming 12 months. Then, generate your name with a new piece of paper together with the adhering to message and Do what it requires to stay the lifestyle you aspiration of! Remember in the end Consistency Wins!

THANK YOU FOR READING!

FEEL FREE TO SHARE YOUR THOUGHTS ON

FARID@ALEEDEX.COM